Monster Giggles

Written by Ken Ross
Illustrated by David Mostyn

FUNFAX™

First published in Great Britain
by Funfax Ltd., an imprint of
Dorling Kindersley Limited,
9 Henrietta Street,
London, WC2E 8PS
This edition published in 2000.
All rights reserved.

THE MUMMY MAKER ...

Why does every soccer team have a monster? Because they all have a ghoulkeeper.

Heard about the monster who soaked his top half in candle wax? He wanted to be wicked.

Why are monster babies less revolting than their parents? Because they are just a little ugly.

Why don't giants like polo? Because they prefer po-high.

YOU SAW A HEADLESS MONSTER IN THE GRAVEYARD?

YES, HONEST. AND IT WAS WEARING GLASSES.

MONSTER GIGGLES

... by Erskin Binder

There is no mistaking the Yeti.
It has dandruff as big as confetti.
It has huge teeth like spears
And blows fire from its ears
And is married to a Yeti called Betty.

The beast of beastly Beast Hall
Is pleased when pedestrians call.
He invites them to dine
And gives them strong wine
Before eating them skin, bone and all.

MAN-EATING TIGERS ...

A monster with eleven feet went into a shoe shop and asked for five pairs of shoes.

The assistant gave him five pairs of shoes, then asked why he was leaving his eleventh foot uncovered.

THAT'S FOR TYING THE LACES

4 MONSTER GIGGLES

... by Stripey Muncher

WHAT NECK OF THE WOODS DO YOU COME FROM?

BOLTON.

TUTOR: How do you know he was an alien?

STUDENT: He said he was from another univers-ity.

CAN I BE SPOTTY, TOO?

HOW DO YOU SPOT A MONSTER?

WITH A PAINT BRUSH

Heard about the monster who fell in love with a bee?

He became a honey monster.

THAT GIVES ME A BUZZ!

MARTIANS ON EARTH ...

Heard about the devil who kept failing his driving test? He couldn't get rid of his hell plates.

FAILED!

Why can't a monster's head be 12 inches wide? Because then it would be a foot.

RIDING LICENCE, MADAM?

Heard about the witch who got booked for travelling too fast on her broomstick? She had a brush with the law.

MONSTER GIGGLES

... by Dave Landed

What do you call a ghost in the fire-brigade? A fire-frighter.

How did the ghost start his letter of complaint? "Tomb it may concern..."

What do ghosts play at parties? Hide and Shriek, then Haunt the Thimble.

CAN I HAVE AN ALSATIAN FOR MY SON?

SORRY, WE DON'T EXCHANGE GOODS.

PHEW!

WAITING FOR SPOOKS ...

Why did you punch him in the nose?

It was the bogeyman.

What does the Invisible Man call his mum and dad?

Transparents.

I DON'T KNOW!

HA! HA! HA!

I'm having quite a hair-raising experience.

What do you mean?

I'm turning into a werewolf.

8 MONSTER GIGGLES

... by X. Spectre

An earth-sucking monster from space
Sucked soil from his own planet's face.
He came here a hero
But sucked a volcano
And erupted all over the place.

There was a young monster called Fred,
Who always ate biscuits in bed.
His mother said, "Son,
That's really not done!
Why don't you eat humans instead?"

KILLER MONSTERS ...

MONSTERS' MENU

Egg, chips and human beans
Shepherd's eyes
Steak and kids' knees pies
Beans on ghost
Cornishman pasty
Babies and mash
The living and onions
Fish and chaps
Tom's heart in soup
Stu and dumplings
Ma'am laid on toast
High scream cornets
Pineapple chumps

Please leave tips
(preferably whole fingers)
in the tray.

AAAAAAAAAAAARGH

... by Des Troyers

What do you say when a monster gets angry? "No need to bite my head off."

What do monsters play at parties? Swallow my leader.

What time is it when a monster sits on your fence? Time to get a new one.

WHERE ARE YOOOOOOOO?

Why can't spectres see very well? Because they don't wear spectrecals.

MONSTER GIGGLES

POWDERED SKULLS ...

TOP TEN JOBS FOR MONSTERS

1. Traffic warden
2. Dentist
3. Dinner lady

HMM! YES! I THINK I'VE GOT A TUMMY ACHE!

4. Doctor
5. Grave digger
6. Head teacher

7. Great Aunt Elspeth
8. Prison officer
9. Caretaker
10. Librarian

... by Ed Bonecrusher

There was a young monster from Harwich,
Who behaved very badly at her marriage.
She proceeded on skates
To the parish church gates,
While her groom followed on in the carriage.

There once was a monster from Leith
Who had most remarkable teeth;
They were ever so strong
And spiky, and long
And he kept each one wrapped in a sheath.

STRETCHING CORPSES ...

What do you give a monster with big feet?

Plenty of room.

What's the definition of a skeleton?

Bones with the people scraped off.

What do you call a witch who goes to the beach but won't go in the water?

A chicken sand-witch.

Where do you find monster snails?

On the end of monsters' fingers.

Why shouldn't you keep a two-headed monster?

Because it costs twice as much to feed.

... by Ivor Longbody

A cannibal monster went on his holidays. When he returned, he had both legs and both arms missing...

... "What happened?" asked a concerned friend. "Oh nothing," said the cannibal monster, "it was a self-catering holiday."

Heard about the monster who ate lamp posts? He stood around on roadsides feeling light-headed.

MONSTER GIGGLES

ALIEN INVASION ...

Heard about Dracula's new boat? It's a blood vessel.

The tooth fairy left 20p under a baby vampire's pillow.

Mummy vampire complained over the stingy amount.

"If that's all the fangs I get, I won't bother next time," said the tooth fairy.

Did you hear about the monster who ate a sofa and two chairs? He had a suite tooth.

16 MONSTER GIGGLES

... by Warren Globe

What do you call a monster who's black and blue all over? Bruce.

What do you get if you cross a monster with a canary? A big yellow thing that goes 'tweet'.

TWEET

MAN: Doctor, I've an insatiable appetite for corpses.
DOCTOR: Has any body noticed?

What do you call a monster that's small and attractive? A failure.

MAN: I keep robbing graves.
DOCTOR: And what does Graves think about this?

SCARING PEOPLE ...

What's big and ugly and has red spots?

A monster with measles.

What's big and ugly and bounces?

A monster on a pogo stick.

What's big and ugly and has wheels?

A monster on roller skates.

I wish you would stop frightening that boy.

Honest, I never spook to him!

18 MONSTER GIGGLES

... by B. A. Devil

WHAT MONSTERS DON'T LIKE ABOUT THE HUMAN WORLD:

- **CAMERAS** - they snap back.
- **ZEBRA CROSSINGS** - it is cruel walking on them.
- **SPOT CREAM** - makes humans taste oily.
- **COMPUTER GAMES** - show monsters as monstrous.
- **SLIPPERS** - they are always too small.
- **NEEDLES** - find them difficult to thread.
- **REMOTE CONTROLS FOR TVS** - buttons too small.
- **CHRYSANTHEMUMS** - can't pronounce it.
- **FAST FOOD SHOPS** - don't sell wildebeest.
- **WRIST WATCH WEARERS** - watch straps get stuck in teeth.
- **SKINNY HUMANS** - need too many for a decent meal.
- **CHILDREN** - who cry when being eaten.
- **RUBBER GLOVES** - seem like fearsome creatures.
- **PINEAPPLE CHUNKS** - tins hard to chew.
- **MONSTER MOVIES** - not real monsters in starring roles.

DON'T WAKE THE GHOST ...

TRUE OR FALSE?

The first monster ever to be captured by humans was known as The Seven Headed Serpent of Stratford.

During the reign of Queen Elizabeth I a reward of twenty-five pigs was offered to any citizen who could capture a living monster. Jonathon Snort, who lived two houses away from the great playwright William Shakespeare, is said to have trapped the beast in 1598. He dug a huge pit in a wood near Stratford-upon-Avon and waited by the pit for almost a month. One evening, when he was near to quitting his all-night vigil, a hideous cry came from the pit.

Jonathon Snort called locals to investigate and, when daylight fell, the people of Stratford-upon-Avon discovered a hideous serpent with, they claimed, seven heads.

YE UGH!

Later it was confirmed that the creature only had four heads, and its screams were a result of it having extremely bad teeth. Days later the monster died after a local man gave it a self-invented cure for toothache.

Jonathon Snort was made a lord, and when he died in 1613, he was buried next to the monster on a hill overlooking Stratford.

The awful truth? I don't think so. There are no hills in Stratford. Or are there...?

20 MONSTER GIGGLES

... by Elsie Wails

> Why don't monsters get measles? Because they have no weak spots.

> Why can't monsters ski? Because they are abominable snowmen.

> "Here's a good book," said the sales assistant to Mrs Monster. "It's called How to Help your Husband get Ahead."

> "Ooh no," said Mrs Monster, "he's got two heads already."

> What did Dr. Frankenstein say when his monster couldn't do simple arithmetic? "You haven't got the brains you were born with".

MONSTER GIGGLES 21

MIDNIGHT IN THE GRAVEYARD ...

An enormous monster with eight arms and eleven legs walked into a tailor's shop.

"Quick!" yelled the tailor to his assistant, "hide the 'Free Alterations' sign!"

What do you do if a monster feels sick? Stand well back.

What do you get if you cross an owl with a monster? A bird that's ugly but doesn't give a hoot.

MONSTER GIGGLES

... by B. Ware

MONSTER GIGGLES

MONSTER HUNT ...

Tarzan was swinging through the jungle one day, when he swung high above the canopy of trees into an evil cesspit of horror. He was surrounded by his worst nightmares - goblins, spooks, trolls, yetis - every hideous, evil-smelling creature you could imagine. Do you know what he said? "Oops, wrong joke..."

I don't know what to make of my husband these days.

How about a casserole?

24   MONSTER GIGGLES

… **by Luke Sharp**

TAUNTING MONSTERS ...

Why do my friends call me a vampire?

Just eat your soup before it clots.

What's a vampire's favourite food?

Leeches and scream.

What are Dracula's girlfriend's favourite jewels? Tomb stones.

What has webbed feet and fangs?

Count Quackula.

Who is the best vampire maths teacher? Counter Dracula.

... by Yul B. Sawry

What's the first thing a monster has to eat when it's had its tonsils out? The doctor.

Why do witches ride broomsticks? Because vacuum cleaners haven't got long enough cords.

Where do American Indian ghosts live? In creepy teepees.

How do monsters have their eggs? Terri-fried.

MONSTER GIGGLES

CALMING WEREWOLVES ...

What's big, red and ugly?

What's scary and used for writing essays? A ballpoint monster.

An embarrassed monster.

What's big, red and has four wheels? A monster in a mini.

What do you get if you cross a fridge with an angry monster? A nasty cold.

What do you do if you find a monster in your bed? Sleep somewhere else.

MONSTER GIGGLES

... by Justin Casey-Howells

MONSTER ROLL-CALL

EILEEN monster with one leg longer than the other

RUSSELL monster walking on leaves

DOUG a monster-gardener

OSCAR an acting monster

BOB a monster who can't swim

CLIFF a monster with a seagull on his head

DOUGLAS a retired monster-gardener

BEATRIX a monster balancing 3 pints of beer on her head

WANDA a sleep-walking monster

HAZEL a nutty monster

SHAUN a bald monster

MONSTER GIGGLES

BONES IN THE GARDEN ...

I get a stabbing pain in my eye whenever I drink tea.

Have you tried taking the spoon out of the teacup?

What walks backwards through walls going "Er, boo"? A nervous ghost.

What's round and bad tempered? A vicious circle.

... by Doug Upskull

A great hairy monster from Datchet
Attempted to shave with a hatchet.
When his nose he did sever
He said "Now I'll never
Have nasal catarrh - I can't catch it."

A monster who lived in the Amazon
Tried to put nighties of his grandma's on.
The reason was that
He was far too fat
To be able to fit <u>his</u> pyjamas on.

HAUNTED HOUSE ...

An archaeologist and his son came across a tomb in a pyramid, thousands of years old. The archaeologist opened the tomb to reveal an ancient embalmed body.

"What's that?" asked the son.
"A mummy," replied the archaeologist.
The son looked puzzled, "If that's a mummy, then where are her kids?"

... by Hugo First

"She's not just a pretty face, you know!"

MONSTER GIGGLES 33

A STRANGE PRESENCE ...

... by Gibbs D. Jitters

A bright red monster named Rudolf was sitting at home gazing out of the window.
"I want to play golf, but rain's stopped any chance of that," he moaned.

His wife bustled in. "It's not even rain, I'm afraid, darling," she said.

"Yes it is!"   "No, it's not!"

"Yes, it is, Rudolf the Red knows rain, dear."

LIFE AS A WEREWOLF ...

Monsters are reasonable house guests
Although neighbours may find them alarming
But if kept in bow ties and string vests
They often are looked on as 'charming'.

OH! HOW SWEET!

A vampire who needs to keep drinking
Sucks blood by the gallon upstairs.
A mummy that's rotten and stinking
You can hide under cushions and chairs.

... by Heir E. Face

If you've found that your ogre wrecks gardens,
And your savage eats neighbouring dogs,
You can offer your neighbour your pardons
And complain of HIS son keeping frogs.

But if your wolf, ghoul, fiend or horror
Takes a dislike to those next to you
And devours them in night-times of terror
Well, there's nothing more you can do...

THE WORLD'S SCARIEST BEAST ...

A ghost teacher was showing her pupils how to walk through walls. "Now did you understand that, class?" she asked. "Because if not, I'll go through it again."

How do monsters protest? They go on demonsterations.

Where do monsters go on holiday? Zombia.

Why do monsters have wavy hair? They drink sea water.

38 MONSTER GIGGLES

... by A. Savage

MY LIFE AS A POLTERGEIST ...

Heard about the bloke who, one night, washed his hair in pea juice because he wanted to become the Pea Rinse of Darkness?

What age did you live in then?

The Band Age.

What did the wizard say when offered two brides? Witch shall I have?

MONSTER GIGGLES

... by I. Flingham

"Mum, why do I have to clean my teeth?"

"I've told you both before..."

"It's to stop us getting bat breath."

"There is a monster in my soup."

"Sorry, sir - that bowl is for the creature on the next table."

GHOST WATCHING ...

FRANK ANSWERS FROM MONSTER FRANK ANKLECHEW

Q: Is it true that monsters hate people?

A: No. Usually we just eat children. We don't care for old wrinkly skin.

Q: What do monsters do in their spare time?
A: Go ballroom dancing and dye their hair green.

Q: Where do monsters live?

A: In wardrobes, under beds, and especially in parents' bedrooms. Kids' beds are too small to sleep in.

... by Luke About

Q: Why do monsters frighten humans?
A: If we didn't, we'd be on the dole.

Q: Do monsters like jokes?
A: Yes. Chomp!
(remainder of questions asked without interviewer's head)

Q: When will monsters take over the world?
A: About ten past seven.

Q: Do monsters ever wear clothes?
A: We wear batman costumes, and sometimes bowler hats.

Q: Finally, what would you like to say to children?
A: Put some salt & vinegar behind your ears, and maybe have a jar of salad cream ready. You'll taste better.

MONSTER GIGGLES

FOREST AXE-MURDERS ...

After midnight Mrs Monster was woken suddenly. Her husband was eating a huge animal in the bedroom ...

For goodness sake, what are you doing, Horace Monster?

... Horace put down the half-eaten animal.

Go back to sleep, love - I'm just having a night-mare.

... by Bury & Underwood

TOP TEN HUMAN MONSTERS

1. P.E. teachers
2. *Strict parents*
3. Nosy neighbours
4. *Park keepers*
5. School caretakers
6. Aunties with whiskers
7. *Sweet shop owners*
8. Brothers and sisters
9. Kids who have everything
10. *Former best friends*

ALL ABOUT VAMPIRES ...

The monster that swims in Loch Ness
Is often seen in a dress.
A reporter asked "why?"
The monster's reply:
"I wouldn't need to if I was photographed less".

A werewolf whose hair kept on growing
Put on clothes but the hair kept on showing.
Finally, in despair,
To lose all his hair
He laid on a lawn needing mowing.

MONSTER GIGGLES

... by Goodblood & Drinket

Many years ago a huge shoal of plaice was swimming in an ocean near a tiny island. A mummy and a daddy plaice became separated from the shoal, and as they were finding their way back they discovered a baby monster struggling in the current.

The mummy and the daddy plaice rescued the monster. They took him back to the shoal, and there he lived happily for twenty-five years. Then one day he suddenly realised he was different. He went to his adoptive parents and asked them why he wasn't flat and silvery like they were. Why, after all this time, hadn't they told him the truth?

Mummy looked at daddy, then she looked at the monster.
"Son," she said softly, "we didn't want you to feel out of place."

MONSTER GIGGLES

A HORRID DEATH by Barry De Lyve

48 MONSTER GIGGLES